a Jim Pattison Company

Consultant Camilla de la Bedoyere
Design Rocket Design
Reprographics Juice Creative

Published by Ripley Publishing 2013
Ripley Publishing, Suite 188, 7576 Kingspointe Parkway
Orlando, Florida, 32819, USA

10 9 8 7 6 5 4 3 2

Copyright © 2013 by Ripley Entertainment, Inc.
Reprinted in 2013
All rights reserved. Ripley's, Believe It or Not!, and Ripley's
Believe It or Not! are registered trademarks
of Ripley Entertainment Inc.

ISBN 978-1-60991-082-2

Manufactured in the USA
in November/2013
2nd printing

Library of Congress Cataloging-in-Publication Data

Fun facts and silly stories 2.
    pages cm. -- (Ripley's believe it or not!)
  ISBN 978-1-60991-082-2
1. Curiosities and wonders--Juvenile literature.
AG243.F855 2013
032.01--dc23

2013019620

No part of this publication may be reproduced in whole or in part, or stored in a retrieval system, or transmitted in any form or by any means, electronic, mechanical, photocopying, recording, or otherwise, without written permission from the publisher.

For information regarding permission, write to
VP Intellectual Property
Ripley Entertainment Inc.
Suite 188, 7576 Kingspointe Parkway
Orlando, Florida 32819

Email: publishing@ripleys.com

www.ripleybooks.com

PUBLISHER'S NOTE
While every effort has been made to verify the accuracy of the entries in this book, the Publishers cannot be held responsible for any errors contained in the work. They would be glad to receive any information from readers.

WARNING
Some of the stunts and activities in this book are undertaken by experts and should not be attempted by anyone without adequate training and supervision.

...Believe it or not!

Wee hee!

Hey guys, wait for us!

Little Wonders

Willard Wigan's sculptures are so tiny he uses a hair from a fly as a paintbrush!

He once made Alice in Wonderland and breathed her in by mistake!

Beauty and the Beast on a pinhead

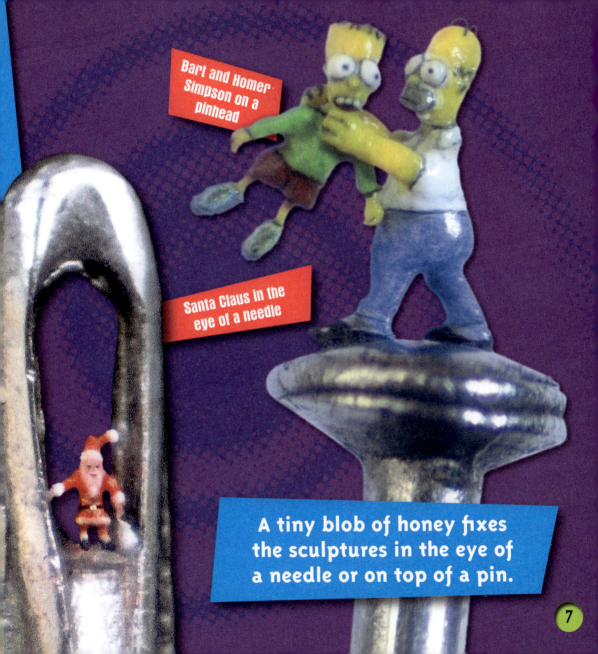

Bart and Homer Simpson on a pinhead

Santa Claus in the eye of a needle

A tiny blob of honey fixes the sculptures in the eye of a needle or on top of a pin.

Some frogs FREEZE during winter then UNFREEZE in summer!

Wood frogs have antifreeze-like blood so they can freeze and then thaw with their surroundings.

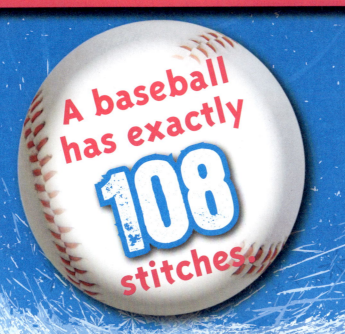

A baseball has exactly **108** stitches.

Snorkel..

Mask.....

A stinking, muddy trench....

At the World Bog Snorkeling Championships in the UK, competitors jump into trenches full of mud wearing snorkels and flippers. They then wade through the course without using swimming strokes, and the fastest through the sludge wins!

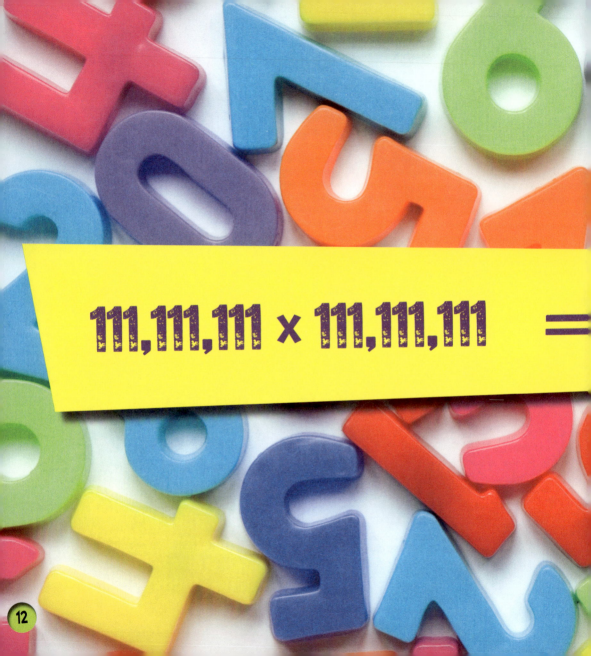

IT'S TRIPLETS!

This is what happens when bananas go **bananas!**

A man in China peeled this banana and found three inside.

Grapes EXPLODE if you microwave them

An average woman wearing lipstick will manage to lick off and eat **one whole lipstick** in her lifetime.

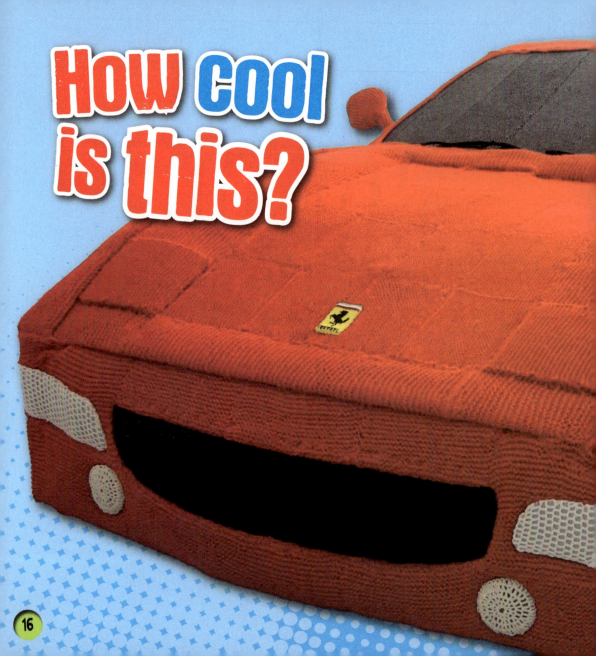

How cool is this?

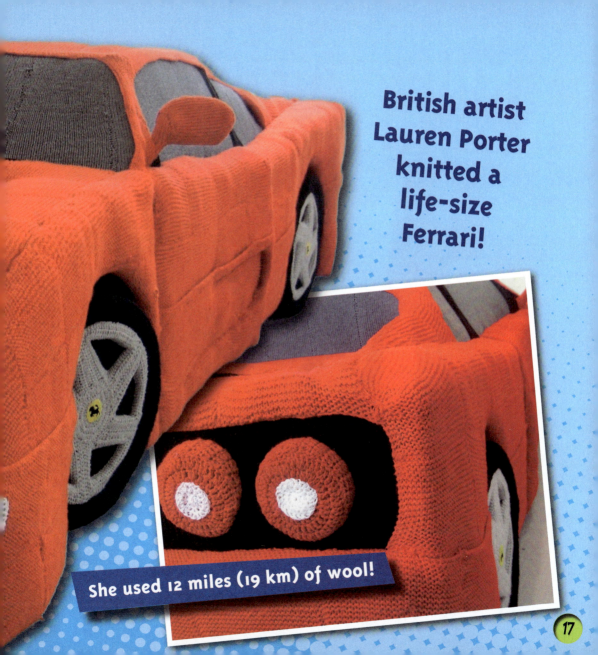

British artist Lauren Porter knitted a life-size Ferrari!

She used 12 miles (19 km) of wool!

Killer whales breathe together.

Point those noses, girls!

When swimming in a group, they all rise to the surface at the same time.

Everyday the world's population flushes away 27,000 trees-worth of toilet paper.

There are mice on Mercury!

Not really, but don't these craters on planet Mercury look like Mickey Mouse's face?!

Astronauts can't cry properly in space because there's no gravity to make tears fall.

If you could smell in space, you might find it smells like a gas station or a barbecue.

OUCH!

One of the world's most poisonous mammals is the

DUCK-BILLED PLATYPUS!

It has a spike on its back leg that injects venom and causes extreme pain.

HEY, PIGS DO FLY...

and candy and motorcycles too...
in these wacky hot-air balloons.

A piece of paper CAN be folded in half more than EIGHT times!

In fact, the record for folding a piece of paper in half is **13** times!

There are **842** separate languages in Papua New Guinea.

A South Korean grandmother failed 949 written tests before getting her driver's license.
Then she had to pass the practical exam!

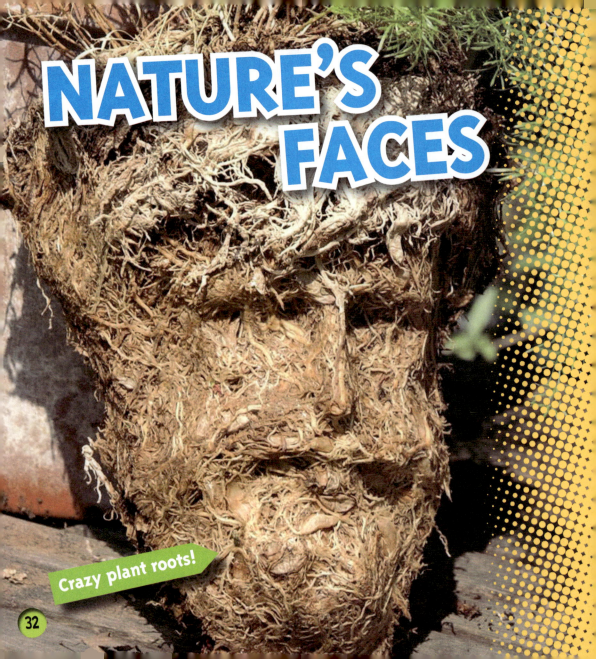

NATURE'S FACES

Crazy plant roots!

32

If you yelled for one year, seven months, 26 days, 26 minutes, and 40 seconds you would make enough sound energy to heat one cup of coffee.

Australia has 23 million people and 120 million sheep!

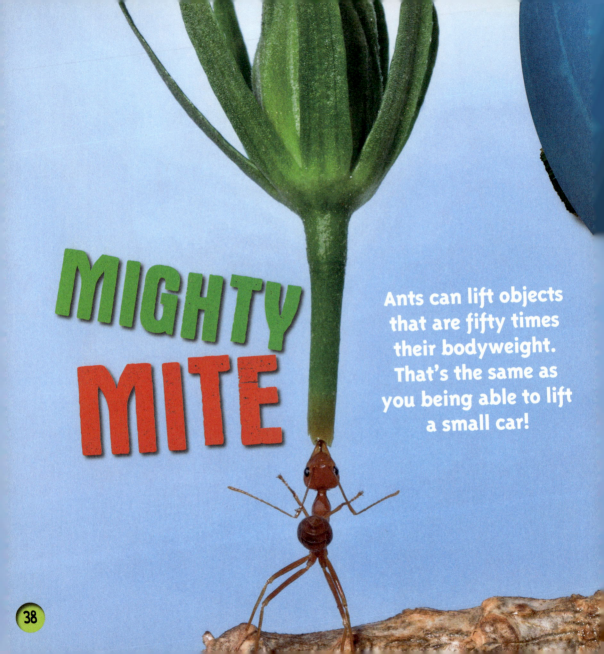

MIGHTY MITE

Ants can lift objects that are fifty times their bodyweight. That's the same as you being able to lift a small car!

There are no ants in Antarctica.

FIRE ANTS CAN SWITCH OFF TRAFFIC LIGHTS!

THEY LOVE CHEWING THROUGH ELECTRIC WIRE SO MUCH THAT THEY ONCE MANAGED TO SWITCH THEM OFF.

WHO GOES THERE?

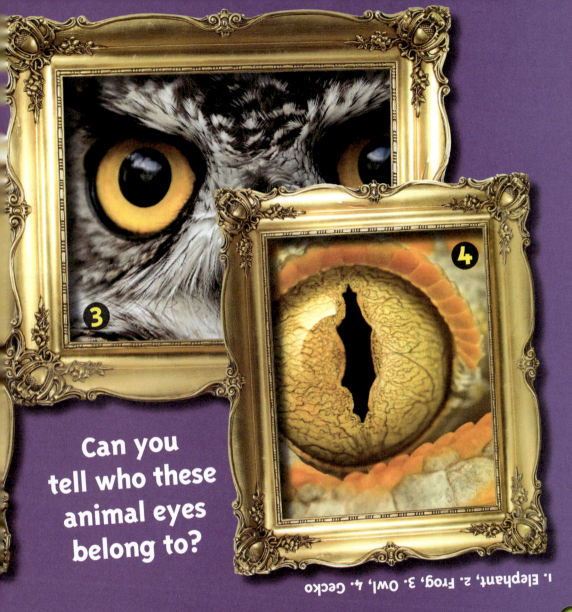

Can you tell who these animal eyes belong to?

1. Elephant, 2. Frog, 3. Owl, 4. Gecko

A group of kangaroos

Flies taste with their legs.

Do they have cheesy feet?

A blue whale's tongue weighs more than an elephant.

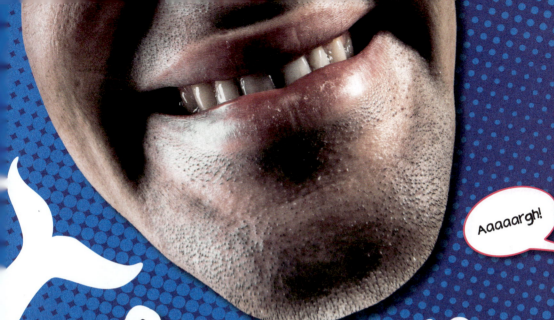

He's flopped!

An inflatable monkey was covered with 10,000 flip-flops in a park in Brazil by Dutch artist Florentijn Hofman.

2,893,500 of the cells in your body will die and be replaced with new cells in the time it takes you to read this line.

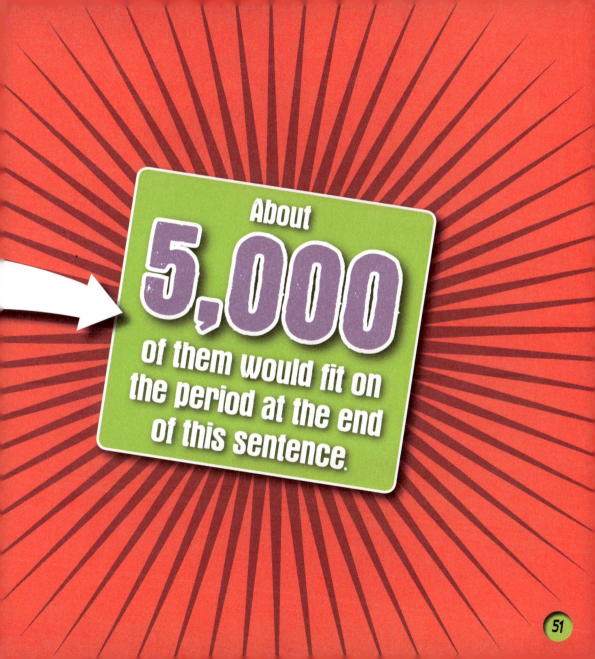

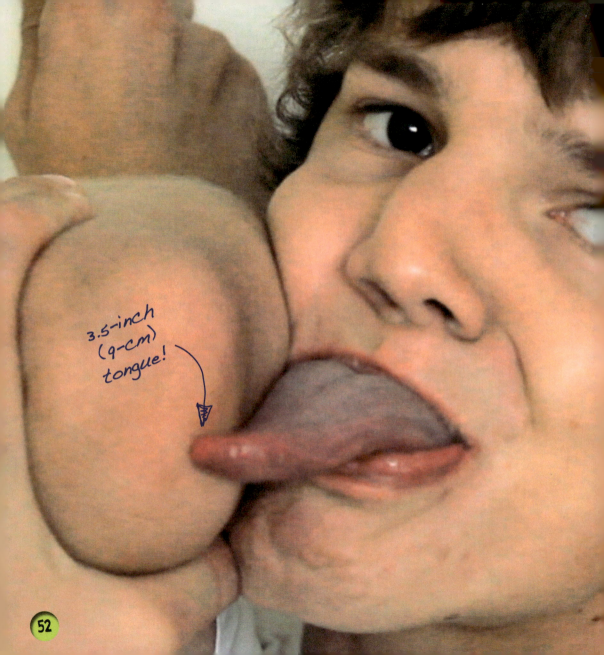

Can you lick your elbow? Try it!

Most people can't. However, Nick Afanasiev can lick his elbow easily because he has a really long tongue!

Smiling takes one more muscle than frowning.

A BANANA SKIN WILL SHINE YOUR SHOES.

Trapped Wind

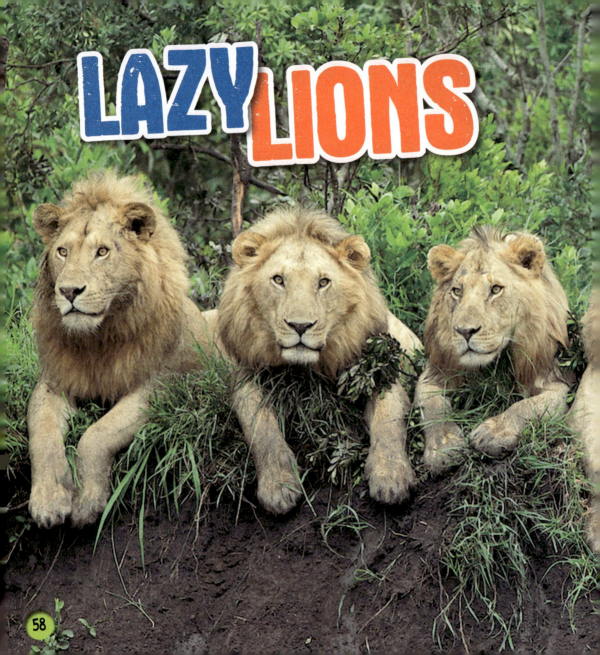

A cuttlefish's eyes have pupils shaped liked a W.

The dot over the letter "i" is called a **TITTLE**.

PIRATES BELIEVED EARRINGS IMPROVED THEIR EYESIGHT.

Land ahoy!

Where? ...hang on, I can't see a thing without my earrings.

Ugly Bugs Close Up!

62

Gary Craig pulled on **302** pairs of underpants in 2012.

There are 43,252,003,274,489,856,000 possible patterns you can make with a Rubik's Cube.

Your stomach grows a new lining every three to seven **days.**

"Quick, take it off John, the cops are coming!"

It is against the law for a driver to be blindfolded while driving a car in Alabama.

A leech has two brains.

"I'm still a low-down, dirty blood sucker!"

Arachibutyrophobia
is the fear of peanut butter sticking to the roof of the mouth.

It takes about 540 peanuts to make a small jar of peanut butter.

WORLD'S SMALLEST PAIR OF SHOES

Each shoe measures 0.15 inches (3.8 mm) long, 0.7 inches (1.8 mm) wide and 0.9 inches (2.2 mm) high.

When you **sneeze**, germs and dirt fly out of your nose at **35 mph** (56 km/h).

Drinking too much water can **kill** you.

Wolf eels are called the UGLY old men of the sea.

But not to their face—their bite is strong enough to crush crabs!

We may be ugly, but we've got each other.

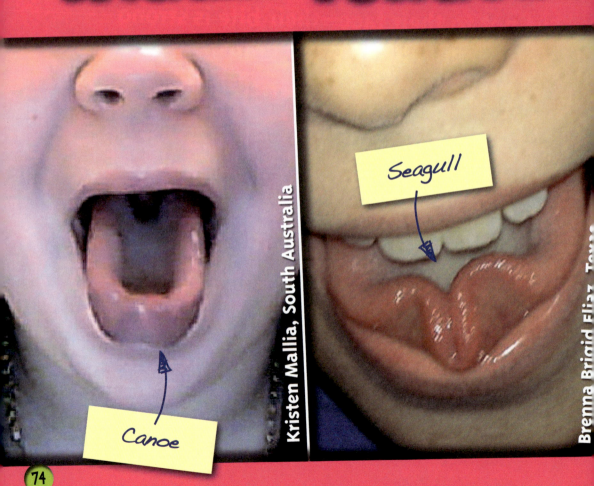

Readers sent us pictures of the crazy tongue shapes they can make.

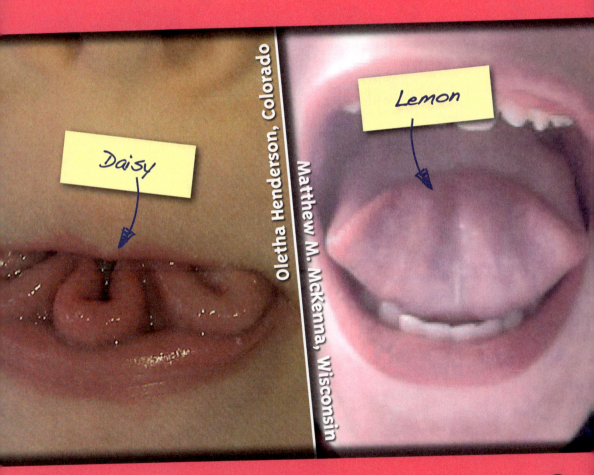

Daisy

Oletha Henderson, Colorado

Lemon

Matthew M. McKenna, Wisconsin

And they're off!

zzzz-zzz

Oh no, my ears just clapped!

76

Pigs with knitted jockeys strapped to their backs race at a fair in Northern Ireland.

Up, Up and Away

Kayleigh O'Connor loves the film *Up* so much that she's decorated her nails with a whole scene from it. On her thumb, a house floats from a bunch of balloons. Her fingernails resemble sky, complete with fluffy clouds.

An average pencil will write about 50,000 words before running out.

Baby octopuses are about the size of a flea when they are born.

CRAZY ABOUT POKÉMON

Lisa Courtney has more Pokémon than anyone else in the world!

They've taken over her home in England. She's so obsessed that she regularly travels to Japan, where the video-game character was created, to collect the latest models.

Do polar bears dance?

No... this one was trying very hard to stand up and was just a bit wobbly rather than groovy!

Crayfish have teeth in their **stomachs** and kidneys in their **heads**.

A BLINK LASTS ABOUT 0.3 SECONDS.

AND THE WINNER IS...

the first person to eat a pie without using their hands!

Guzzle

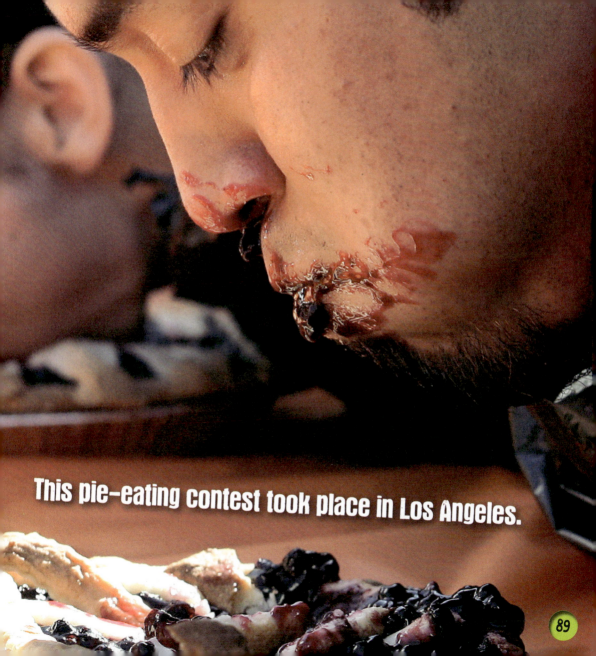
This pie-eating contest took place in Los Angeles.

Nicholas Peake, a teacher from England, has been coughing up to **100 times an hour for 15 years!**

20 volcanoes are erupting right now!

MUTANT KILLER PENGUINS!

Penguins can bend their heads all the way back to scratch their own backs! They have double-jointed necks, which help them get to any hard to reach places.

Wooooo!

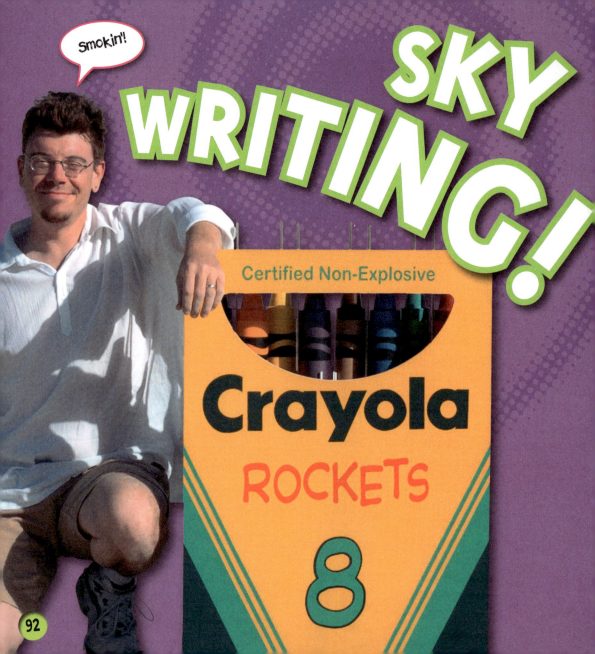

John Coker's hobby is building rockets. He designed eight as a giant box of crayons and, after six years of planning, took them to the Nevada Desert to set them off.

Only four crayons flew, but they reached 2,928 feet (892 m).

This number, with 100 zeros, is called a googol.

10,000,000,000,000,000,000,000,000,000,000,000,000,000,000,000,000,000,000,000,000,000,000,000,000,000,000,000,000,000,000,000,000,000,000,000,000,000,000

CUBISM

This portrait of SpongeBob SquarePants is made out of 150 Rubik's Cubes. Josh Chalom needed 30 helpers to twist Rubik's Cubes to show the correct patterns for the picture.

A frog has to blink to swallow!

Blinking pushes its eyeballs down on top of its mouth and pushes food down its throat.

Your body produces half a gallon of gas each day in BURPS AND FARTS!

Pharp...

Oh dear, pardon me!

THERE'S A TOWN IN NORWAY CALLED "HELL"

OWLS HAVE 3 EYELIDS

FOWL PLAY

Jim?

No, it's Dave

Whose smart idea was this?

A Chinese farmer came up with special glasses for his chickens to stop them fighting. The glasses stop the chickens looking straight ahead—and now they don't fight.

BEST HOOF FORWARD

Sprout, a miniature horse from Colorado Springs, wears shoes!

The tiny horse volunteers at the local hospital—bringing a smile to people's faces—but after falling over on the slippery floor, his owner, Gretchen Long, tried some teddy bear sneakers for size. Now, he can trot around the hospital without a stumble!

SOME CLOUDS WEIGH AS MUCH AS 85 ELEPHANTS!

In China, fish and chips are served with **sugar.**

yuk!

Tasty Face

Every day for a **whole year** American artist James Kuhn painted his face with a different design.

Some of his designs were food themed, such as these burger, popcorn, and pineapple faces.

SPIDER SNACK

- 🕷 Take one black tarantula.
- 🕷 Fry in hot oil with salt and sugar.
- 🕷 Top with wafer-thin garlic slices.
- 🕷 Serve as a snack in Cambodia.

Eeww, gross!

COWS HAVE ACCENTS

Farmers in England have said that their cows have different moos depending on which herd they come from.

cor blimey Guv!

PRETTY POOL

Lake Hillier in Western Australia is pink and no one knows why.

Even when the water is taken away in a container, it's still pink!

There are two golf balls sitting on the Moon.

They were hit by American astronaut Alan Shepard when he walked on the Moon in 1971.

It's a Whopper!

There are ten fields of these giant mushrooms in China.

When farmer Rong Guiling bought the seeds, she was told the mushrooms would be small white ones!

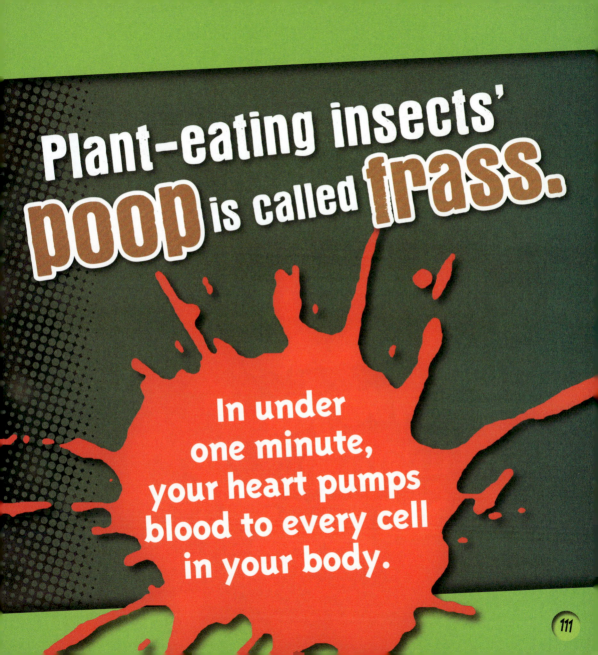

A tick eats just **3** times in its life.

Cockroaches can live for a month without food.

Do unicorns exist?

Massive? How rude, it's distinguished.

No, but there are unicorn fish. They have a massive horn at the front of their head.

SPLOOOSH!

Erghh, that's gonna whiff!

"Milking" is the new craze in the U.K.

Take one four-pint container of milk.
Stand in a public place.
Pour milk over head.
Take a video and post on YouTube.

You share your birthday with at least **19 million** other people.

CREEPY CRAWLEY

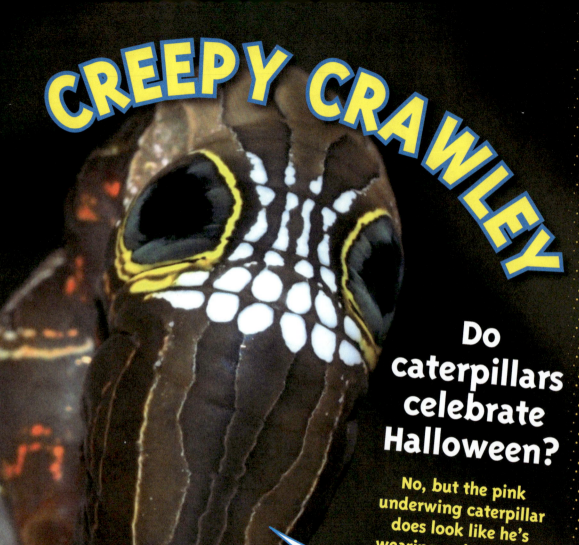

Do caterpillars celebrate Halloween?

No, but the pink underwing caterpillar does look like he's wearing a skull mask!

Trick or treat?

The fear of **Halloween** is called Samhainophobia.

Horned lizards squirt **blood** from their eyes. They do it to defend themselves.

BIG DADDY

Bigfoot 5 has the largest Monster Truck wheels ever!

SWEET DREAMS

Seven pandas were born within three months of each other in a sanctuary in China in 2012. They got to have a sleepover!

A cow can drink a  **bathtub** of water in one day.

Each inch of a human armpit has just over **half a million** bacteria.

Euwww!

Barking MAD!

What's doga? It's yoga for dogs and their owners, of course! Classes take place in Crystal Beach, Florida.

I'd rather chase a stick in the park!

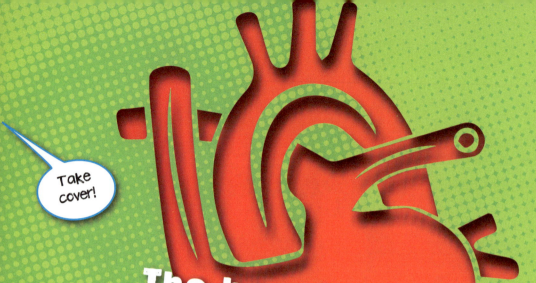

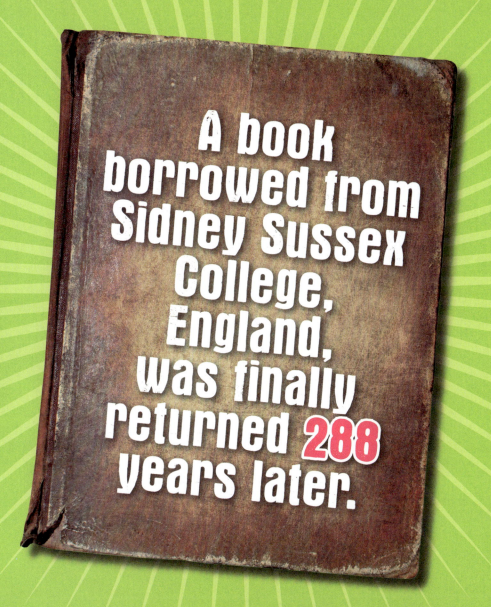

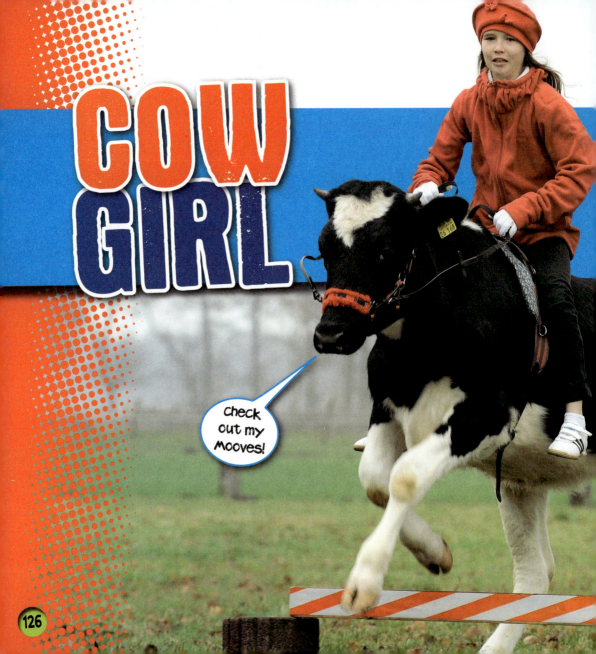

When her parents said no to a horse, Iris Becker learned how to ride a cow.

Americans Brian and Steve Seibel played table tennis without stopping for 8 hours 15 minutes and 1 second in 2004.

They hold the world record for hitting the ball back and forth to each other without dropping it or stopping.

Spiders have **CLAWS** at the end of their legs.

Barbie dolls in Japan are now made with their lips closed and have no teeth.

HOT water freezes faster than COLD water.

Your fingernails take about six months to grow from the base to the tip.

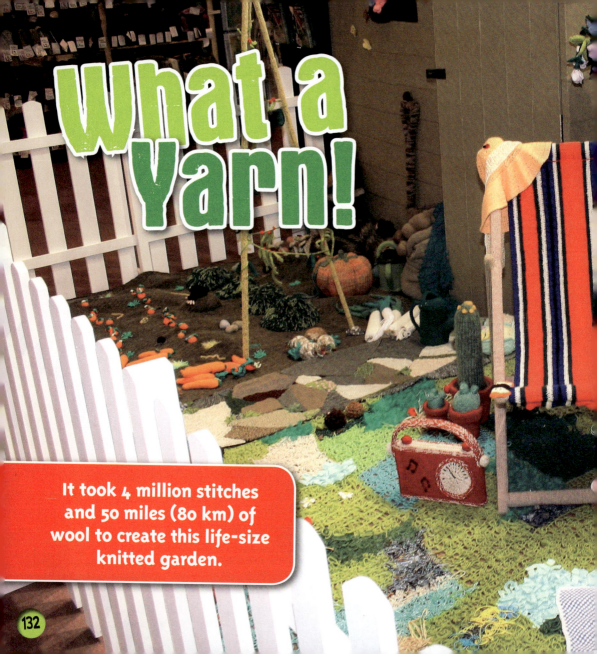

What a Yarn!

It took 4 million stitches and 50 miles (80 km) of wool to create this life-size knitted garden.

Golden Grin

Sebastian, a black Persian cat, has two gold crowns on his bottom teeth.

Now you die... Mr Bond!

His teeth stuck out, so the crowns were added for strength.

A clam taken from the sea north of Iceland was

405 years old!

There is a breed of dog with TWO noses!

The double-nosed Andean tiger hound is a hunting dog with an excellent sense of smell.

An **eyelash** lasts for approximately 75 days before falling out.

Some bamboo plants grow **3 feet** (0.9 m) in 24 hours.

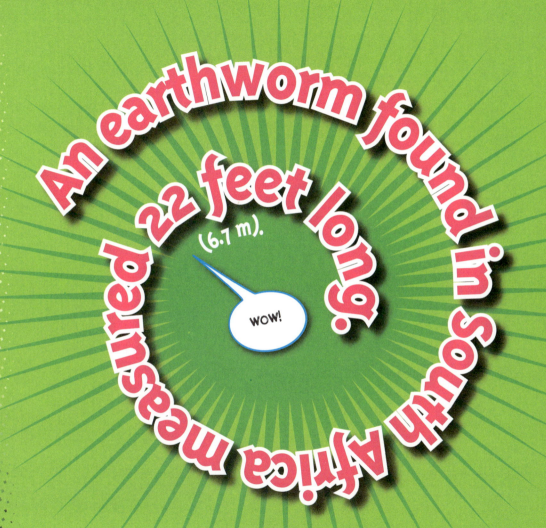

DOGS DRIVE CARS!

Yes, they really do! In New Zealand, dogs are being taught to drive cars to prove how clever they are. Monty, Ginny, and Porter learned how to move the gearshift, accelerator, brake and steering wheel.

How Much?

A woman in Thailand spent **$16,240** on a wedding for her cat.

The body of the average baby is 75% water.

When porcupines are mad they stomp their feet!

oooo... get you!

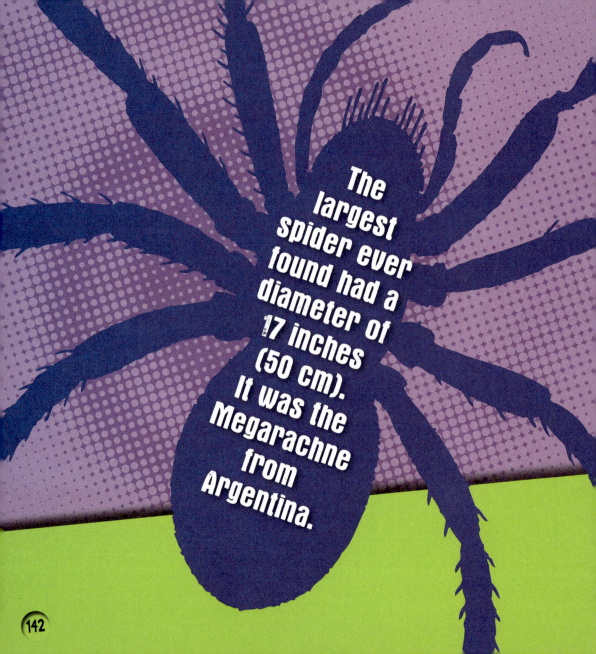

An average person uses the toilet **2,500** times a year.

Roy C. Sullivan, from Virginia, was struck by lightning **seven** times between 1942 and 1977.

FREAKY TEETH

Give us a kiss!

BABIRUSA
Upper canines pierce the skin of its upper jaw and grow through the skull.

144

NAKED MOLE RAT

Digs with its teeth and seals its lips behind them to stop soil getting inside.

VAMPIRE BAT

Front teeth shave hair from its prey, then cut the skin allowing it to drink blood.

EGGPLOSION!

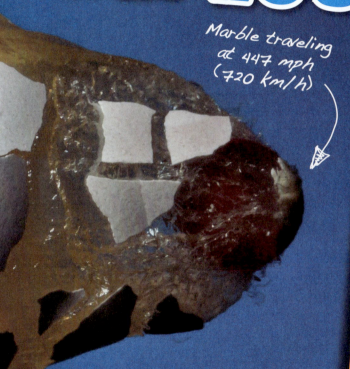

Marble traveling at 447 mph (720 km/h)

Look what happens when you fire a marble at an egg and take a picture!

Lemons contain more sugar than strawberries.

Roughly one out of every 55 Canadian women give birth in their car on the way to the hospital.

Just drive Gordon!!

Look, it's a greater spotted warbler!

Pizza Problem?

Breakfast: Pizza
Lunch: Pizza
Dinner: Pizza
Snacks: more Pizza!

Sophie Ray has eaten nothing but plain pizza for the last eight years—even a slice of pepperoni is enough to turn her stomach!

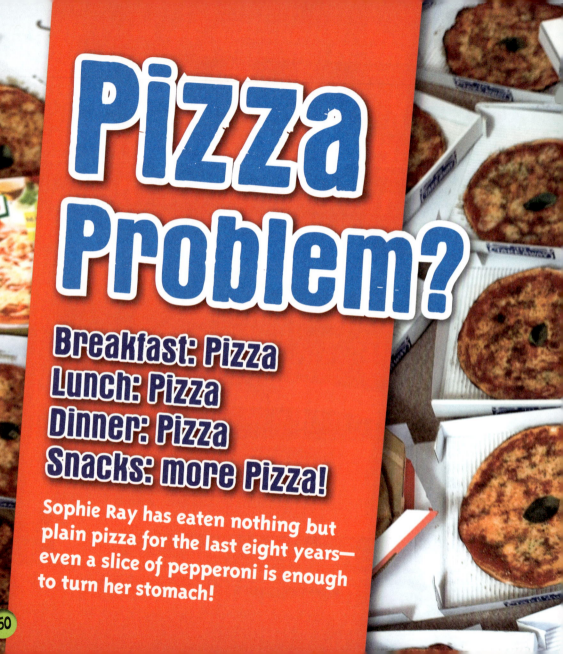

Sticky Pictures

Ben Wilson paints on chewing gum stuck to the streets of London.

Look where you step, I've only just painted that!

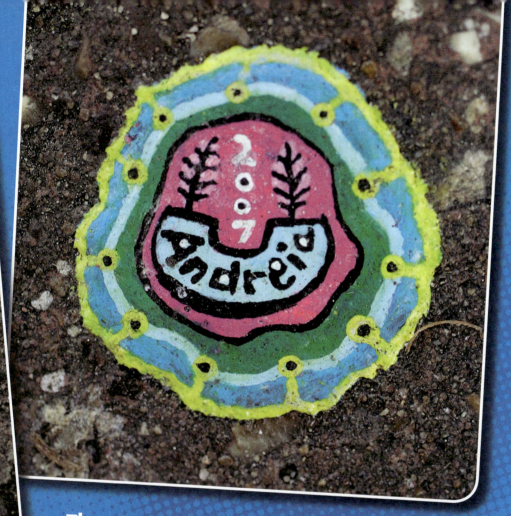

There are thousands of the tiny artworks all over the city—you just have to know where to look!

You have a unique tongue print.

Like fingerprints, it can be used for identification.

How did you find the cake thief, Sarge?

The accused left their tongue prints all over it, sir.

One in ten people lives on an island.

There are more plastic flamingos in the United States, than real ones!

ENGLISH

The big breakfast at Jester's Diner, in the U.K., weighs the same as a small child. **So far, no one's finished it!**

Papakolea Beach in Hawaii has **green** sand.

Randy Gardner went without sleep for 264 hours 12 minutes in 1964.

Afterward, he slept for just 14 hours 40 minutes.

BATS HAVE THUMBS.

Believe it or not, you can't eat this dinner. It's an oil painting made by Tjalf Sparnaay from the Netherlands.

CHEEKY CHOPS

Hey, watch this.

A chipmunk's cheeks are three times bigger than its head... when stuffed.

LONELY LIFE

An elderly couple in China refused to allow their house to be knocked down... so a new road had to be built around it.

A blue whale makes a noise louder than a jumbo jet.

A crocodile can spend up to an HOUR under water without breathing.

It manages to do this by slowing its heart rate down to two or three beats a minute.

Gasp!

Chameleons can look forward and backward at the same time! Each eye can move independently.

Hey, I've got my eye on you...

...and you!

Joann Osterud flew an aircraft upside down for **4 hours 38 minutes 10 seconds** over Canada in 1991.

The Hawaiian alphabet has only **12** letters.

Neck Ache!

37.5 inches (95 cm) long

Lurch, a Watusi bull from Arkansas, had the world's biggest horns.

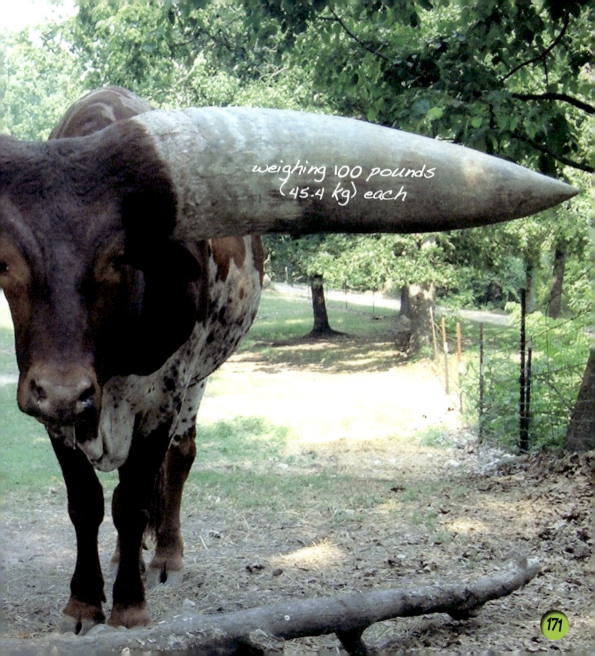

You May Now Kiss the Robot...

I-Fairy, a robot, helped out at this wedding in Tokyo, Japan. It was the first wedding in the world to be led by a robot.

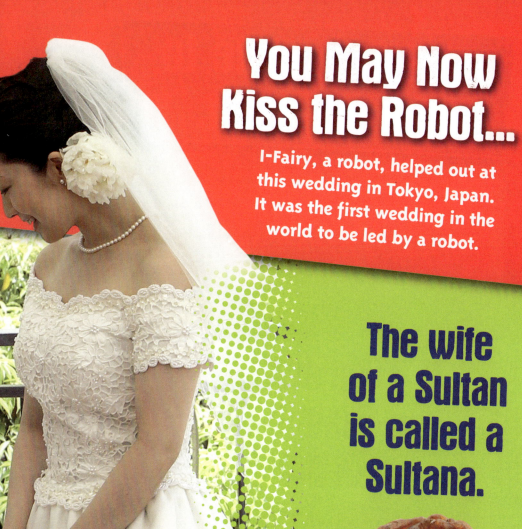

The wife of a Sultan is called a Sultana.

It's impossible to tickle yourself. Try it!

One part of your brain warns the rest of your brain that you are about to tickle yourself. Since your brain knows this, it ignores the tickle.

Good job too if you ask me!

Elephants are the only mammals that can't jump.

No words in the dictionary rhyme with orange.

He's NUTS!

Sammy the squirrel spends hours playing the piano!

He lives in England with piano teacher Shirley Higton and started disturbing her lessons by scampering all over the keys. He has now been bought his own instrument.

SUCH FUN!

Derek never takes hunting seriously

The mouth of a hyena is so tough it can chew through a **GLASS BOTTLE** without cutting itself.

After spotted hyenas have caught their prey they celebrate by making a noise that sounds like a **GIGGLE.** This alerts the other hyenas to come and share the food.

HEAD IN THE CLOUDS

Fancy staying here? These giant figures of three Chinese gods are actually a hotel in Beijing, China.

You Must Be Yoking!

A cook was amazed to crack open seven eggs one after the other and discover they were all double-yolked!

An egg with two yolks is so rare, you might have to crack open a thousand eggs to find one.

SPARKLING RIDE

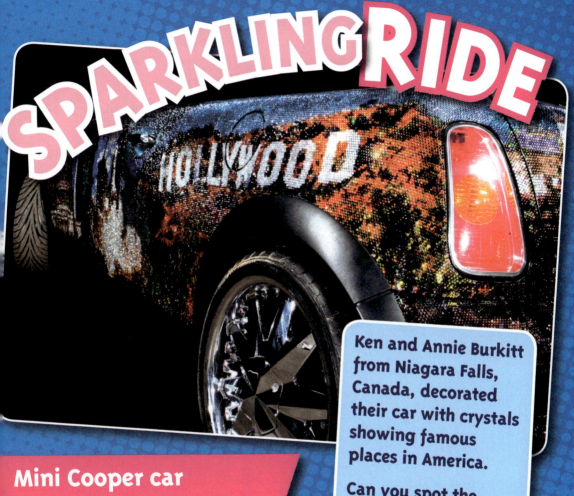

Ken and Annie Burkitt from Niagara Falls, Canada, decorated their car with crystals showing famous places in America.

Can you spot the Statue of Liberty?

Mini Cooper car covered in more than one million crystals!

Beach Monster

This mighty mosaic dragon on a beach in China is made from 900 tents!

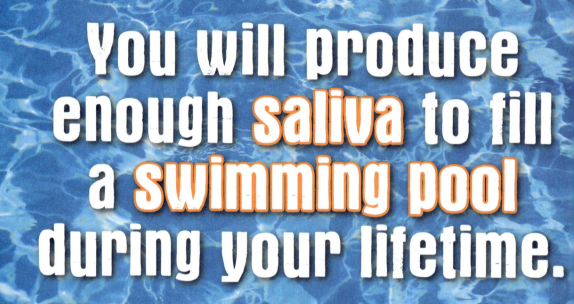

A shrew's heart beats 1,000 times a minute...

...but an elephant's beats only around 30 times a minute.

Your brain does not feel pain.

It can send out pain signals to the rest of your body, but the brain itself does not actually feel pain.

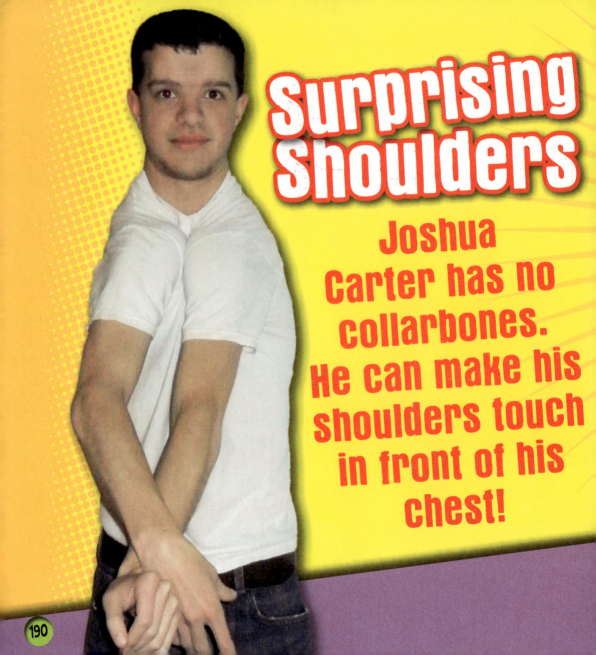

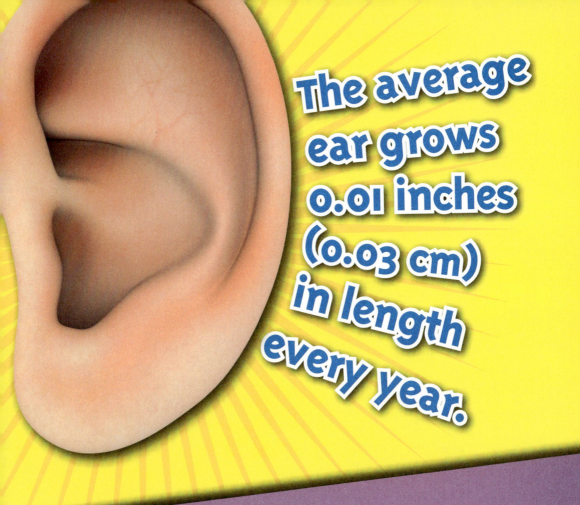

The average ear grows 0.01 inches (0.03 cm) in length every year.

The distance between your elbow and your wrist is the same length as your foot.

> In Ancient Rome, bald men often painted hair onto their scalps.

QUIRKY QUARTET

Oleksandr Bozhyk can play four violins at once!

Birds don't sweat.
They have no sweat glands.

3 babies are born in the world every second.

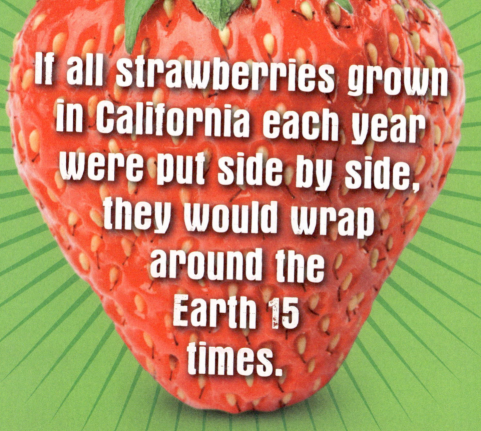

If all strawberries grown in California each year were put side by side, they would wrap around the Earth 15 times.

HOUSE MUSIC

Every time it rains, the pipes that cover this building in Dresden, Germany, become a giant musical instrument and play a tune.

Barry Yip from Hong Kong once spent 81 hours and 23 seconds singing 1,000 karaoke songs.

The chances of giving birth to identical triplets is 1 in 200 million.

Giraffe hooves are as big as dinner plates.

SKY SURFER

This cloud over England looks more like a dolphin than rain.

200

Babies don't cry.

They don't shed tears until they are about 8 months old—when their tear ducts are fully developed.

DOZING DRIVER

Masik the squirrel was found abandoned as a baby and was nursed back to health. He is so devoted to the man who found him that he even dozes on the steering wheel while his owner drives!

It is against the law to take a **LION** into a cinema in Baltimore, Maryland.

Aaarghh

Run for your lives!

Honeybees beat their wings about 11,500 times a minute!

Your body sheds around 500,000,000 flakes of skin every day.

Really gross!

RAINBOW BURGER

- Take two quarter pounders—one yellow, one blue.
- Add orange, green, and scarlet beef slices.
- Include some peacock-blue cheese.
- Add purple lettuce.
- Dribble on purple and orange mayo.
- Squeeze between a sesame bun.
- Enjoy!

BUG-POPS

Er, I'm fine thanks.

You can buy lollipops filled with disgusting insects! Edible, a company based in the U.K., created the bug-pops using lots of different insects, including worms, scorpions, and ants.

rminate!

A couple in California dressed up their Christmas tree as a Dalek, the fictional alien in the British TV series *Dr Who*.

SEEING RED

I am not paddling in that!

The sea turned red in 2012 at Clovelly Beach, Sydney, Australia.

The blood red water was caused by algae (tiny plants) growing in the sea.

The world's biggest snowflake was 15 inches (38 cm) wide and 8 inches (20 cm) thick. It fell in Montana in the U.S.A. on January 28, 1887.

Take cover!

The human body has about 60,000 miles (97,000 km) of blood vessels.

That's the same distance as 2½ times around the world!

Your nails would grow to about 13 feet (4 m) long if you never cut them.

You can buy a perfume that smells like cheese.

"You smell lovely tonight darling, is it that new "cheese" perfume?"

"No, it's my feet."

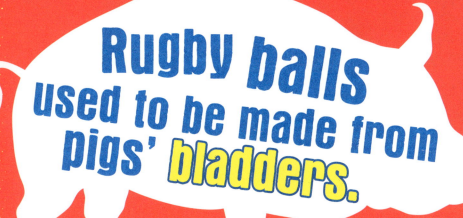

Rugby balls used to be made from pigs' bladders.

You take about 600 million breaths in a lifetime, that's about **23,000** breaths a day!

A bubblegum bubble 20 inches (51 cm) across was blown by Chad Fell from the U.S.A.

Major League baseball teams use about **850,000** balls each season.

Golf balls used to have **HONEY** in the middle.

Mmm, very tasty!

INDEX

A
aircraft 169
alphabet 169
ants 38-39
armpits 122
astronauts 23, 108

B
babies 141, 149, 194, 201
baldness 193
balloons 56-57
bananas 14, 55
Barbie dolls 129
baseballs 9, 219
bats 158
Bigfoot 118-119
birds 194
birthdays 115
blinking 85
blood vessels 215
bog snorkeling 10-11
books 125
brains 109, 189
breakfast 156-157
breathing 217
bugs 62-63, 209
burgers 206-207

C
cars 16-17, 184-185, 198
caterpillars 116
cats 134, 140
cells 50-51
chameleons 168
chickens 99
chins 47
chipmunks 162-163
Christmas tree 210-211
clams 135
clouds 101, 200
cockroaches 112
collarbones 190
coughing 90
cows 106, 122, 126-127
crayfish 85
crocodiles 166
cuttlefish 60

D
dinner painting 160-161
dogs 122-123, 135, 138-139
driving 29, 67, 138-139, 202-203

E
eagles 84
ears 191
eggs 146-147, 182-183
elbows 52-53, 191
elephants 174
eyelashes 136
eyes 40-41

F
faces 32-33, 102-103
fish 34-35, 113
fish and chips 101
flamingos 155
flies 46
frogs 9, 97

G
gas 97
giraffes 36, 199
golf balls 108, 219
googol 94-95
grapes 15
gum 152-153, 218

H
hairs 167
Halloween 116-117
hearts 111, 124, 189
honeybees 205
horses 100
hot-air balloons 26-27
hotels 180-181
houses 164-165, 196
hyenas 178-179

I
ice cream 71
insects 111
islands 154

J
jaguars 180
jawfish 207
jellyfish 6, 44, 175

K
kangaroos 42-43
knitted garden 132-133

L
lakes 106-107
languages 29
leeches 67

220

lemons 148
lightning 143
lions 58-59, 204
lipstick 15
lizards 117

M
mass gatherings 44-45
Mercury 22
mice 25
"milking" 114
monkeys 48-49
Moon 108
moustaches 30-31
mushrooms 110
music 196

N
nails 78, 131, 215
Norway 98
numbers 12-13

O
octopuses 79
owls 98

P
pandas 120-121
paper-folding 28
peanut butter 68-69
pencils 79
penguins 91
perfume 216
phobias 47, 68, 117
pie-eating contest 88-89
pigs 8, 76-77, 86-87, 217
pirates 61

pizzas 150-151
plants 136
platypus 24
Pokémon 80-81
polar bears 82-83
poop 111
porcupines 141
Professor Splash 20-21

R
rabbits 148
robots 172-173
rockets 92-93
rubber bands 130, 159
Rubik's Cubes 65, 96

S
saliva 188
sand 157
sculptures 6-7, 48-49
sea 212-213
seagulls 84
seals 34-35
sheep 37
shrews 189
shoes 70
singing 197
skin 205
sleep 25, 158
smiling 53
sneezing 72
snowflakes 214
space 23
spiders 104-105, 128, 142
squirrels 54, 176-177, 202-203
stomachs 66

strawberries 195
Sultana 173

T
table tennis 127
teeth 144-145
tents 186-187
tickling 174
ticks 112
tittles 61
toilet paper 19
toilets 143
tongues 52, 74-75, 154
toys 198
triplets 197

U
underpants 64-65

V
violins 192-193
volcanoes 90

W
water 131, 141
Watusi bull 170-171
whales 18-19, 46, 165
wolf eels 73
word rhymes 175
worms 137

Y
yelling 37
yoga 122-123

PHOTO CREDITS

COVER: Reuters/Cathal McNaughton (front); Phil Rees/Rex Features (back)

4-5 Geckoeye.com; **8** © afhunta - iStock.com; **9** (sp) © Helena_Ogorodnikova - Shutterstock.com, (b) © Albo - Fotolia.com; **10-11** Phil Rees/Rex Features; **12-13** © Glen Coventry - iStock.com; **14** HAP/Quirky China News/Rex Features, (b) © Preto Perola - Shutterstock.com; **18-19** (dps) AFP/Getty Images; **19** (c) © Andrew Buckin - Shutterstock.com; **20-21** Michael Martin/Barcroft Media Ltd; **22** NASA/Johns Hopkins/Carnegie/Rex Features; **23** © Nicemonkey - Shutterstock.com; **25** © Photoshot; **26** David Bagnall/Rex Features; **26-27** Susan Montoya Bryan/AP/Press Association Images; **27** David Hartley/Rex Features; **28** © nuttakit - Shutterstock.com; **30-31** Reuters/Vincent Kessler; **32** Rex Features; **33** (l) Geoffrey Robinson/Rex Features; (r) Ken Laverty/Bournemouth News/Rex Features; **34-35** © David Fleetham/naturepl.com; **36** Paul Goldstein/Rex Features; **37** (t) © Butterfly Hunter - Shutterstock.com, (b) © oorka - Shutterstock.com; **38** Lessy Sebastian/Solent News/Rex Features; **39** (t) © Jacek Fulawka - Shutterstock.com; **40** (l) © Eric Isselee - Shutterstock.com, (r) © Hamady - Shutterstock.com; **41** (l) © Ammit Jack - Shutterstock.com, (r) © B & T Media Group Inc. - Shutterstock.com; **42-43** © William Ross-Jones - istock.com; **44-45** Con/Demotix/Demotix/Press Association Images; **46** © dkvektor - Shutterstock.com; **47** © Aleksey Klints - Shutterstock.com; **48-49** Florentijn Hofman; **50** © Henrik Jonsson - iStock.com; **52** Nick Afanasiev; **54** Polizei GroÃÐburgwedel/DPA/Press Association Images; **55** © saiko3p - Shutterstock.com; **56-57** Leigh Winburn/Rex Features; **58-59** David Dolpire/Solent News/Rex Features; **60** © Bill Kennedy - Shutterstock.com; **62-63** (l, c, r) Eye Of Science/Science Photo Library, (dps) © Kamil Macniak - Shutterstock.com; **64** Picture courtesy of the Shields Gazette; **66** © Kitataka - Shutterstock.com; **67** © Birsen Cebeci - Shutterstock.com, © szefei - Shutterstock.com; **68** © Africa Studio - Shutterstock.com; **69** © Madlen - Shutterstock.com; **70** ©Huang Xiaoyong/Xinhua/eyevine; **71** (t) © LHF Graphics - Shutterstock.com, (b) © M. Unal Ozmen - Shutterstock.com; **72** © Lunarus - Shutterstock.com; **73** © Jeffrey Rotman/Jeff Rotman Photography/Corbis; **74** (L) Kristen Mallia, (r) Bridgid Lednicky; **75** (l) O F Henderson, (r) Matthew M Mckenna; **76-77** Reuters/Cathal McNaughton; **78** Kayleigh O'Connor/Solent News/Rex Features; **79** © Julia Ivantsova - Shutterstock.com; **80-81** Paul Michael Hughes/GuinnessWR/Rex Features; **82-83** © Steven Kazlowski/naturepl.com; **84** © Marcus Varesvuo/naturepl.com; **86-87** ©Stacy Sodolak/Polaris/eyevine; **89** AFP/Getty Images; **91** © Lunarus - Shutterstock.com; **92-93** John Coker/Rex Features; **95** © Umberto Shtanzman - Shutterstock.com; **96** Caters News Agency; **97** © lantapix - Shutterstock.com; **98** © Brad Collett - Shutterstock.com; **99** Quirky China News/Rex Features; **100** © Cate Terwilliger/Polaris/eyevine; **101** © Nata-Lia - Shutterstock.com; **102-103** James Kuhn/Rex Features; **104-105** © Mario Weigt/Anzenberger/eyevine; **106** © Dudarev Mikhail - Shutterstock.com; **107** © Jean-Paul Ferrero/ardea.com; **108** © FrameAngel - Shutterstock.com; **109** © liveostockimages - Shutterstock.com; **110** Quirky China News/Rex Features; **111** © Lunarus—Shutterstock.com; **112** © Ksanawo - Shutterstock.com; **113** BNPS.co.uk; **114** Caters News Agency; **115** © Laborant - Shutterstock.com; **116** Lui Weber/Rex

Features; **118-119** Sipa Press/Rex Features; **120-121** Evens Lee/ColorChinaPhoto/AP/Press Association Images; **122** © Baloncici - Shutterstock.com; **123** © Douglas R. Clifford/PSG/eyevine; **124** © vladis_studio - Shutterstock.com; **125** © Ensuper - Shutterstock.com; **126-127** Action Press/Rex Features; **128** © Photoshot; **130** © Michael Francis McElroy/ZUMA/eyevine; **131** © Aaron Amat - Shutterstock.com; **132-133** ICHF www.ichf.co.uk; **134** Courtesy of David C Steele; **136** © Subbotina Anna - Shutterstock.com; **138-139** DraftFCB New Zealand/SPCA; **140** © kuban_girl - Shutterstock.com; **142** © pio3 - Shutterstock.com; **143** © lukethelake - Shutterstock.com; **144-145** ©Heidi & Hans-Juergen Koch/eyevine; **146-147** Alan Sailer/Rex Features; **148** © Lev Kropotov - Shutterstock.com; **149** © Sako Verife - Shutterstock.com; **150** Caters News Agency; **152-153** © Jon Enoch/eyevine; **155** © Ken Hurst - Shutterstock.com; **157** Caters News Agency; **159** (sp) © Lana B - Shutterstock.com, (c) © lucadp - Shutterstock.com; **160-161** Caters News Agency; **162-163** Solent News/Rex Features; **164** HAP/Quirky China News/Rex Features; **166** © seaskylab - Shutterstock.com; **167** © Inga Ivanova - Shutterstock.com; **168** © TiberiuSahlean - Shutterstock.com; **170-171** Janice M. Wolf; **172** Reuters/Yuriko Nakao; **173** © Pamela Uyttendaele - Shutterstock.com; **174** © Jared Shomo - Shutterstock.com; **176-177** Caters News Agency Ltd; **178** Bridgena Barnard/Rex Features; **180-181** Wenn.com; **182** Emma & Harry Smith-Hughes; **186-187** HAP/Quirky China News/Rex Features; **188** © Igor Kaplunopvich - Shutterstock.com; **190** Joshua Carter; **191** © heromen30 - Shutterstock.com; **192-193** Reuters/Marian Striltsiv; **195** © Maks Narodenko - Shutterstock.com; **196** Exclusive Pix; **197** © SoleilC - Shutterstock.com; **198** AFP/Getty Images; **199** © Yusuf YILMAZ - Shutterstock.com; **200** Matthew Sears/East News/Rex Features; **201** Paul Goldstein/Exodus/Rex Features; **203** Pitor Pankratov/SellYourPhoto.net; **204** © svtrotof - Shutterstock.com; **205** © Africa Studio - Shutterstock.com; **206** By Henry Hargreaves, styled by Lisa Edsalv; **208** Nathan Sawaya, brickartist.com; **210** Caters News Agency; **210-211** © Chris Harvey - Shutterstock.com; **212-213** Newspix/Rex Features; **214** © Euco - Shutterstock.com; **215** © calvindexter - Shutterstock.com; **216** © swinner - Shutterstock.com; **217** © oorka - Shutterstock.com; **218** © Robynrg - Shutterstock.com; **220 & 224** Phil Rees/Rex Features

Key: t = top, b = bottom, c = center, l = left, r = right, sp = single page, dp = double page

All other photos are from Ripley Entertainment Inc. Every attempt has been made to acknowledge correctly and contact copyright holders and we apologize in advance for any unintentional errors or omissions, which will be corrected in future editions.

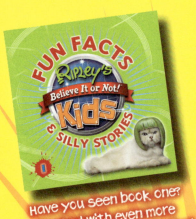

Have you seen book one? Packed with even more fun facts and silly stories!

We hope you enjoyed the book!

If you have a fun fact or silly story, why not email us at bionresearch@ripleys.com or write to us at BION Research, Ripley Entertainment Inc., 7576 Kingspointe Parkway, 188, Orlando, Florida 32819, U.S.A.